dabble lab

DRAW MANGA
MYTHICAL CREATURES

MANGA DRAWING
WITH MERMAIDS, UNICORNS, AND OTHER MAGICAL CREATURES

written by Naomi Hughes
illustrated by Vincent Batignole

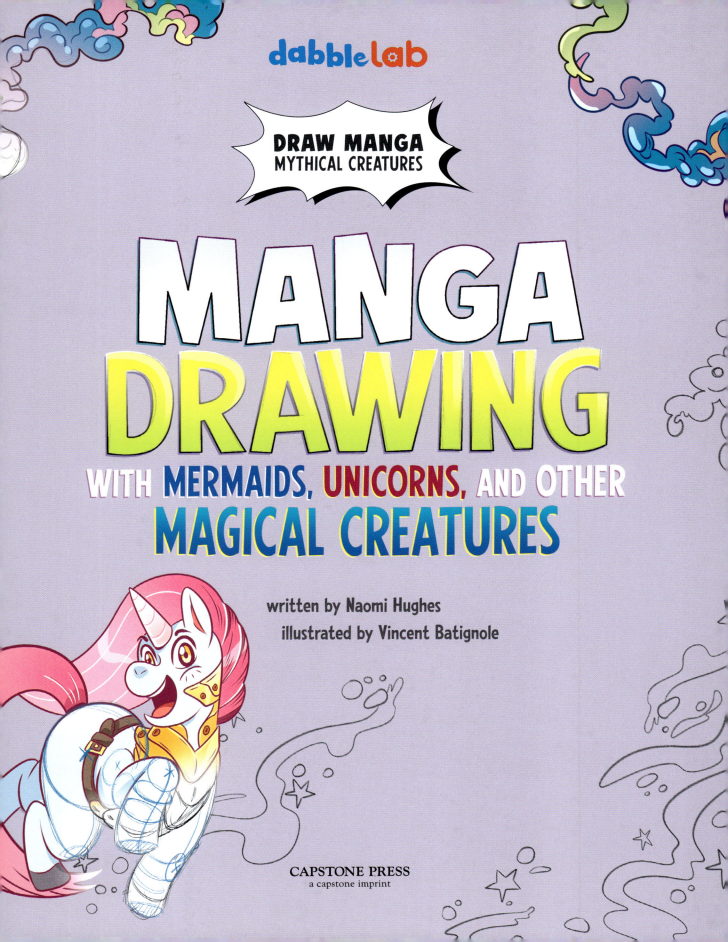

CAPSTONE PRESS
a capstone imprint

Published by Capstone Press, an imprint of Capstone
1710 Roe Crest Drive, North Mankato, Minnesota 56003
capstonepub.com

Copyright © 2026 by Capstone. All rights reserved. No part of this publication may be reproduced in whole or in part, or stored in a retrieval system, or transmitted in any form or by any means, electronic, mechanical, photocopying, recording, or otherwise, without written permission of the publisher.

Cataloging-in-Publication Data is available on the Library of Congress website.

ISBN: 9798875221552 (hardcover)
ISBN: 9798875221514 (ebook PDF)

Summary: Following illustrated step-by-step instructions, artists of all abilities can learn how to draw mermaids, unicorns, and more enchanting magical creatures of myth in the dynamic manga art style.

Editorial Credits
Editor: Abby Cich; Designer: Hilary Wacholz; Production Specialist: Tori Abraham

Any additional websites and resources referenced in this book are not maintained, authorized, or sponsored by Capstone. All product and company names are trademarks™ or registered® trademarks of their respective holders.

The publisher and the author shall not be liable for any damages allegedly arising from the information in this book, and they specifically disclaim any liability from the use or application of any of the contents of this book.

Printed and bound in the USA. 006307

TABLE OF CONTENTS

Magic and Mystery 4

Supplies 5

Mermaid 6

Centaur 8

Cat-Sìth 10

Mandrake 12

Nymph 14

Quetzalcóatl 16

Jinn 18

Unicorn 20

Elf 22

Kitsune 24

Qilin 26

New Friends 28

Draw More Manga Creatures! 32

About the Author 32

About the Illustrator 32

MAGIC AND MYSTERY

What does magic look like?

Maybe it's in the gleam of mermaid scales. Or in the fluffy fox tails of a mystical kitsune. Magic lives in many creatures. Now, you can bring those creatures to life in one of the coolest art styles ever—manga!

Manga is a lot like comics. It tells a story using art. Manga got its start in Japan. But today, it's popular all over the world. From cute animal stories to epic adventures, manga's got tales for everyone.

Manga art has its own style. Artists draw characters in poses full of action and emotion. They can also use special symbols to show mood. Human characters often have large, shiny eyes and small mouths. Don't forget neat hairstyles! Giant hair spikes, bright colors, and more show off spunky personalities. Manga creatures show off, too, with over-the-top features. Monsters are often drawn with lots of angles, like pointy chins and sharp teeth. Cute critters might have big, round faces and sparkly eyes.

Manga is perfect for drawing enchanting mythical beings. So, bring your art supplies and imagination because it's time to try it for yourself.

Get ready to draw mermaids, unicorns, and other magical creatures . . . MANGA STYLE!

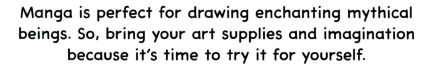

SUPPLIES

Paper. Plain copy paper works well, but many artists use sketch paper.

Pencil. Keep the point sharp (or use a mechanical pencil) and draw lightly. That way, you can easily erase when you need.

Eraser. Because no one draws perfectly all of the time! Plus, manga drawings may take extra practice. Test your eraser first to make sure it doesn't smudge or tear the paper.

Pen. Use a black marker pen with a fine tip or a regular pen. Once you're done with your pencil sketch, trace over it with pen. This will make the lines in your art dark and bold.

Colored markers, colored pencils, or crayons. If you'd like, add color to your art after you've outlined it in pen. Check the ink is dry first so your lines stay crisp.

DID YOU KNOW?
Pro manga artists have special dip pens and ink pots. They use these tools to draw the lines in their final art.

MERMAID

Some sailors say these half-human, half-fish creatures are bad luck. Spotting one means storms and disaster lie ahead. But in Southeast Asia and Ireland, they tell other stories. They say caring mermaids fall in love with humans. If you spy a magical mer-person, count yourself lucky! Though watch out for storms, just in case.

TIP
Mermaids can have different human and fish features. Try drawing one with webbed hands or a super-long tail.

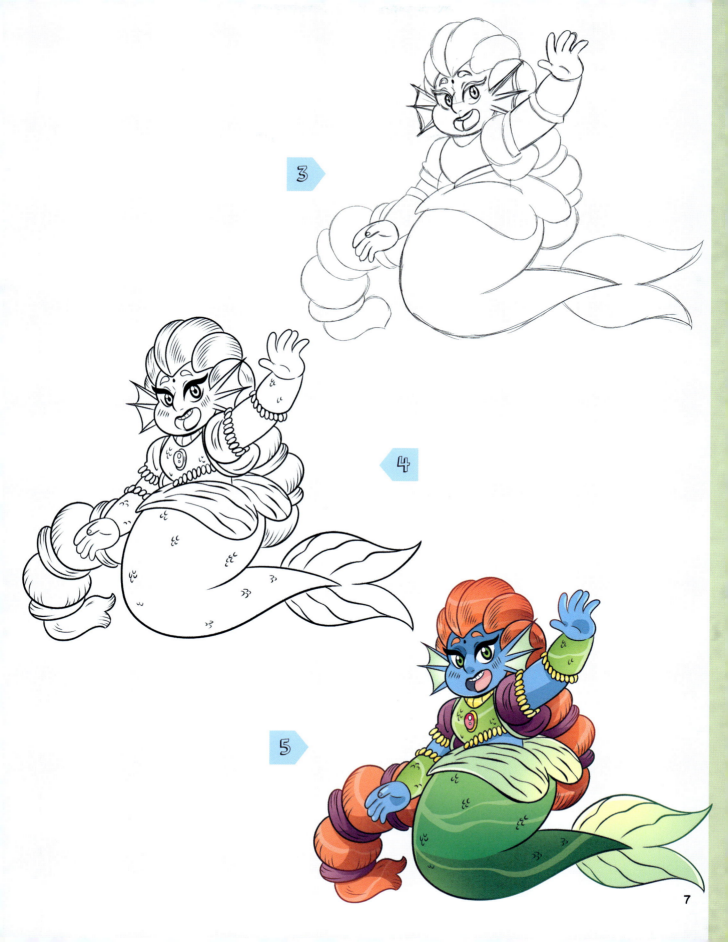

CENTAUR

Centaurs gallop with their strong legs. They can wield a sword with their nimble hands. These human-horse mash-ups have many skills. But one thing they don't have? Good manners! Centaurs often live in wild mountains and forests. Old stories say that they are rowdy and rude.

1

FACT
The Greek centaur Chiron was wise rather than rowdy. He taught many heroes, and even a god.

2

Cat-Sìth

If you catch sight of this critter in the hills of Scotland or Ireland, you might think it's a big cat. But the cat-sìth is no feline. It's a fairy! It stalks through the foggy moors on four paws. And sometimes, when no one is watching . . . it walks on its back feet like a human.

FACT
Some people leave milk out for the cat-sìth. They hope it will bless them with good luck.

MANDRAKE

This plant may look cute, but it packs a toxic punch. Anything that tries to eat it ends up poisoned. And toxin isn't the mandrake's only defense. When this leafy legend is uprooted, it shrieks loudly—really loudly. Stories say its scream can drive a human mad.

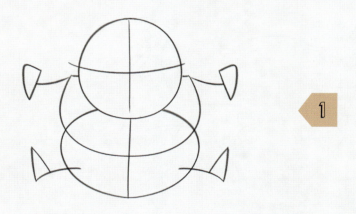

1

> **TIP**
> Want a fancier mandrake? Add colorful berries or big flowers.

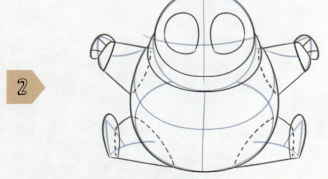

2

12

NYMPH

Kind and beautiful, these gentle spirits are guardians of nature. Nymphs don't wander the land. Each stays put to watch over her own special tree, river, mountain, or sea. They usually appear as young women. Some, though, are very old. There are even tales that say nymphs are ancient goddesses.

FACT
Nymphs were first spotted hundreds of years ago in Greece.

QUETZALCÓATL

It's a bird! It's a snake! No—it's Quetzalcóatl! This feathered serpent has been slithering over the mesas of Mexico since ancient times. The Aztec people honored it as a god. The majestic creature was said to protect crafters and priests. It also has a soft spot for books, writing, and learning.

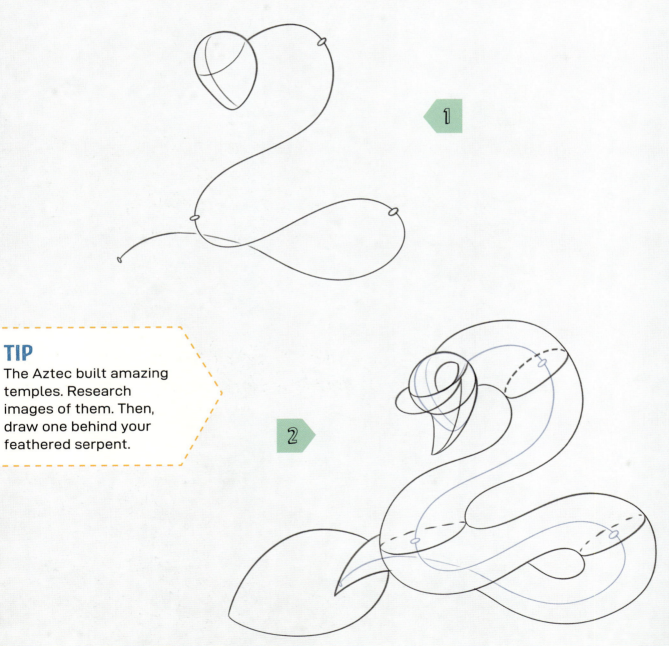

TIP
The Aztec built amazing temples. Research images of them. Then, draw one behind your feathered serpent.

16

Jinn

Old tales say that jinn are spirits made from flame. They can change their shape to look like a human or an animal. They can even turn themselves invisible! If you run into one of these mighty beings, mind your manners. Many can be cruel. They will punish anyone who insults them.

FACT
Jinn have been sighted in North Africa and the Arabian peninsula.

Unicorn

Graceful and strong, unicorns play a part in legends all over the world. They are even the national animal of Scotland! Stories say that unicorns are beasts of purity and innocence. Their horns have healing powers. These enchanting creatures are famously free-spirited. But rumors say they can be tamed by maidens.

1

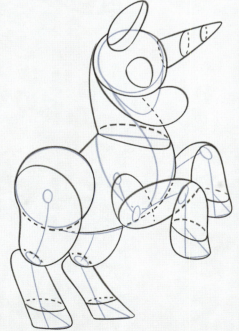

2

TIP
Leave a white dot or two in your unicorn's eyes. This "eyeshine" makes manga characters look cute and sweet.

20

ELF

Many cultures tell tales about these magical beings. In Germany, elves are small and full of mischief. The pranksters replace human babies with elf children. In Iceland, on the other hand, elves are powerful and mystical. They guard nature and remind people to respect the beauty of the land.

FACT
Icelandic elves are called Huldufólk. It means "Hidden People."

KITSUNE

These supernatural foxes come from Japan. Most love to play pranks. They make trouble for humans. But some are helpful. They reward good deeds. Whether tricky or kind, all kitsune possess powerful magic. They can change their form to look like humans—or monsters!

1

TIP
The number of tails shows a kitsune's age. Add more for an older, more powerful fox. Draw fewer for a young one.

2

QILIN

These rare Chinese creatures have a special job. Whenever a wise person is born or dies, a qilin appears to mark the event. With its unique body, it is easy to spot. Dragon scales glitter on its torso. Strong antlers crown its head. It may look fierce. But this grand animal is gentle and noble.

FACT
Qilin are kind to everyone—even to plants! It's said they will refuse to step on fresh grass.

26

NEW FRIENDS

This mermaid loves to dive and play in the ocean. The unicorn spends its days galloping through the forest. These two magical beings come from such different worlds. But they want to be friends! A smile and kelp snack are a great way to start.

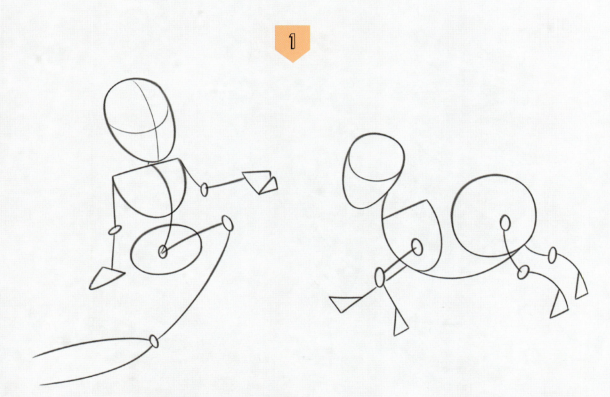

1

TIP
Small diamond shapes can create a sparkly effect. Add them to make the water shine!

28

5

DRAW MORE MANGA CREATURES!

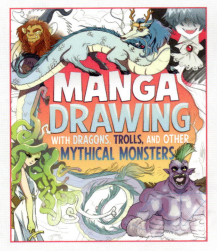
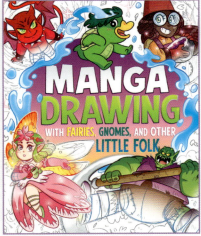
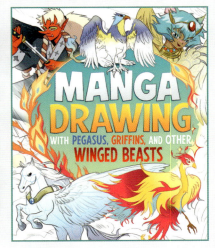

ABOUT THE AUTHOR

Naomi Hughes is an author and school librarian in Minnesota, where she lives with her family and a house full of pets. She writes all sorts of books for kids, from nonfiction picture books to science fiction and fantasy for teens. She loves all things manga and anime and also enjoys traveling, reading, escape games, and going on adventures.

ABOUT THE ILLUSTRATOR

Vincent Batignole trained at the École Pivaut in Nantes, France, and since 2005, has been illustrating and writing for various international clients. He lives in Paris, surrounded by what's easily one of the biggest collections of manga drawn by CLAMP.